COMPOST IT

by David Barker

CHERRY LAKE PUBLISHING • ANN ARBOR, MICHIGAN

Published in the United States of America
by Cherry Lake Publishing
Ann Arbor, Michigan
www.cherrylakepublishing.com

Printed in the United States of America
Corporate Graphics Inc
January 2010
CLSP06

Consultants: Karen O'Connor, co-owner, Mother Earth Gardens, Minneapolis, Minnesota; Gail Saunders-Smith, associate professor of literacy, Beeghly College of Education, Youngstown State University

Editorial direction: Book design and illustration:
Melissa Johnson   Emily Love

Photo credits: Margaret M. Stewart/iStockphoto, cover, 1; Alan Crawford/iStockphoto, 5; Fotolia, 7, 17; iStockphoto, 10; Dorling Kindersley, 12; Lisa Fletcher/iStockphoto, 19; Dennis Oblander/iStockphoto, 21; Arpad Benedek/iStockphoto, 22; Hedda Gjerpen/iStockphoto, 24; Sharon Day/Fotolia, 27

Library of Congress Cataloging-in-Publication Data
Barker, David, 1959-
  Save the planet : compost it / by David Barker.
    p. cm. — (Language arts explorer)
  Includes index.
  ISBN 978-1-60279-656-0 (hardback) — ISBN 978-1-60279-665-2 (pbk.)
  1. Compost—Juvenile literature. 2. Compost—Study and teaching (Elementary)—Activity programs. I. Title. II. Series.

  S661.B367 2010
  631.8'75—dc22

                         2009038092

Cherry Lake Publishing would like to acknowledge the work of The Partnership for 21st Century Skills. Please visit www.21centuryskills.org for more information.

TABLE OF CONTENTS

You are being given a mission. The facts in What You Know will help you accomplish it. Remember What You Know while you are reading the story. The story will help you answer the questions at the end of the book. Have fun on this adventure!

Your mission is to discover the secrets of compost. What is compost? What is composting? Is it something only farmers do? Is it stinky or dangerous? Why do people bother to compost? Why is composting good for the planet and good for us? Keep in mind the What You Know facts as you read.

WHAT YOU KNOW

★ Healthy soil is a mixture of sand, tiny pieces of rock, rotting and rotted plant and animal bodies, and many tiny living things.

★ Bacteria are tiny organisms. They are so small that they can be seen only through a microscope.

★ Some bacteria cause diseases, but many more bacteria help us. There are even some bacteria we couldn't live without.

★ Fungi are plantlike organisms that do not have roots or leaves. Mushrooms and molds are the most familiar types of fungi. Small fungi work in the soil with bacteria.

Some people make compost in their backyards.

★ Compost is put on a garden to nourish the plants that are growing there. It helps plants fight disease. It keeps water in the soil.

A reporter from *Green News* magazine has been sent to interview people and learn more about compost. Carry out your mission by reading her story.

I am deep in the forest with soil ecologist Dr. Jane Robinson. As we walk, she explains: "A soil ecologist learns about the living things in soil. We learn how they work together and what they do."

"What do they do?" I wonder out loud.

"Most are decomposers," replies Dr. Robinson. "They take dead plants and animals and break them down into simple chemicals. It's like eating for them."

A Closer Look

At a clear spot under a large tree, we sit on the ground. Dr. Robinson picks up a clump of leaves from the forest floor. "These are leaves that fell last fall. You can still tell they are leaves. You can even tell which tree they came from," says Dr. Robinson.

Brushing aside this layer, she grabs a handful of brown, crumbly leaf pieces. "These are leaves from the year before. It's hard to tell which tree they came from," she says. "Oh look, here's a beetle and some tiny snails. They are helping to break down these leaf parts. This whole process is called decomposition."

Trees and plants decompose on the forest floor.

Going Deeper

Dr. Robinson digs even deeper. She grabs a handful of damp, black, crumbly stuff that looks like dirt. "This comes from two years ago. This is almost completely decomposed. It's called humus. New plants can get the nutrients they need to grow from humus. How do you think humus is made?" Dr. Robinson asks.

"Good question," I reply. I have no idea.

BREAKING DOWN PLANTS

Plant cells are made in part from the tough threads of a chemical called cellulose. Plants are tough because cellulose is tough. When we eat plants, our bodies cannot break down the cellulose. Only some bacteria and fungi are able to break down the cellulose that plants make.

"Insects, worms, and other larger animals start breaking apart the large parts of fallen plants and dead animals. The work at the end is done by tiny bacteria and other organisms like fungi," she explains.

We Need Decomposition

On the way out of the forest Dr. Robinson adds, "Without decomposition, the world would stop because plants wouldn't have nutrients from which to grow. And animals, including us, wouldn't have plants to eat. Decomposition happens everywhere all the time." ★

I have traveled to Mr. David Singh's backyard. I'm here to see a compost heap in action. Mr. Singh has agreed to help me start my own backyard compost heap.

Compost Box

Mr. Singh's compost is in a large square box. It's about four feet across by four feet deep by three feet high (1.2 m by 1.2 m by 1 m). The box is full of a large pile of leaves, yard clippings, and kitchen scraps. Amazingly, when Mr. Singh lifts the top layer from the heap, steam comes out!

"Touch it," he says. I do, and it's hot! The compost is hot!

HOT AND COLD COMPOSTING

You can compost using either the hot composting or cold composting method. Temperatures inside a hot compost heap can reach 160°F (71°C). The heat is made by special heat-loving bacteria. The hot temperature kills diseases and weed seeds that may be in the material. Cold composting is also called rotting. It is slower, and it won't kill weed seeds.

A wooden box can hold compost.

Why Compost?

"Why do you compost?" I ask Mr. Singh.

Mr. Singh explains that he composts so that he produces less garbage. "Why would you want to make less garbage?" I ask.

"Garbage goes to the city landfill or garbage dump," he replies. "Less garbage means the landfill will last longer. Land for a new landfill is difficult to find and expensive.

A PLACE TO COMPOST

A messy pile can turn into compost. However, it's easier to make compost in a box. A three-sided box of wood, brick, or wire screen works well. The open side makes it easy to turn the compost with a pitchfork. You can also buy a compost container. You can use some types of these containers on a balcony or patio if you don't have a yard.

Composting saves land and it saves everyone money. Also, if we keep making landfills, someday we may run out of land.

"I also compost because it makes my soil better," continues Mr. Singh. "I grow flowers, and Mrs. Singh grows vegetables. The compost improves the soil for our plants. When plants grow, they take nutrients from the soil. Nutrients are the minerals and chemicals that plants need to grow. Just like we need to eat proteins and vitamins, plants need their nutrients. If the nutrients are not put back in the soil, the soil will become less able to grow plants. Compost adds nutrients. Compost also adds bacteria and fungi that make the soil richer." ★

Mr. Singh has come to my backyard. We are building my compost heap. He told me any large container like his box would work. Yesterday I stacked some large bricks to make a three-sided space the size of his box.

Compost Material

I have already collected the things Mr. Singh said we need. First, I gathered a large pile of dead, brown leaves and a large pile of green weeds. I also saved kitchen scraps for a week, leaving out anything with meat, oil, or cheese.

A compost pile needs both kitchen scraps and yard waste to work.

I included coffee grounds, eggshells, and all kinds of vegetable scraps. Finally, I needed a bucket of dark compost from Mr. Singh's compost heap.

I ask why a compost pile needs different ingredients. Mr. Singh replies, "The animals, bacteria, and fungi that live in the compost pile need to have a balanced diet, just like we do."

I ask, "You mean like people need to eat both vegetables and grains?"

Mr. Singh replies, "Exactly! The organisms also need the right balance of nutrients to eat. If there is too little of one nutrient, they will die or grow slowly. This will slow down the composting."

CARBON AND NITROGREN IN COMPOST

Composting requires food for bacteria and other organisms. The food needs two kinds of nutrients. The first is carbon, which is found in brown plant materials including dry leaves and pine needles. The second is nitrogen, which is found in green plant parts, food scraps, and manure. Carbon is the food energy that bacteria, fungi, and even humans need to live. Nitrogen makes up protein, an important building block of all living things.

"Why did you tell me not to compost meat and cheese?" I ask.

"In an outside compost pile, meat and cheese will stink and attract animals you might not want, like mice, raccoons, or the neighbor's dog. Plus, if these materials rot, they may ruin the compost," replies Mr. Singh.

Compost in Layers

On the bare ground inside my box, we add a layer of leaves. Over the leaves, we add weeds and kitchen scraps. Mr. Singh sprinkles some of his compost on top. "Why are you adding that?" I ask.

He replies, "Our leaves, weeds, and kitchen scraps have bacteria and fungi in them but not many. It's not necessary, but adding my compost gets us started with lots of organisms. It will make the composting go faster."

We add another layer of leaves, more weeds, and more kitchen scraps. I ask, "Why are we making layers?"

Mr. Singh explains, "Bacteria and fungi don't move very far. We want them to be able to get to the different nutrients they need. So, we mix the nutrients up for them.

When things get going, we will turn the compost with a pitchfork to mix them even more."

We add more layers until the pile is two feet (0.6 m) high. We have lots of leaves left over, but Mr. Singh says to keep these to add with new kitchen scraps, weeds, or other green plant cuttings. When we finish, Mr. Singh waters the compost heap until it is soaking wet. ★

WATERING YOUR COMPOST

The bacteria and fungi in a compost pile need water to live. A compost pile should be as wet as a squeezed-out sponge. The organisms also need oxygen, like we do. The compost should be loose, or it should have holes poked in it. If oxygen cannot reach the center of the compost pile, the pile will start to smell bad. This is a sign that the pile is too wet or that it needs to be turned over.

We come back two weeks later to check on the progress of my compost heap. Mr. Singh puts his hand inside the heap and nods. I put my hand inside, too. It feels warm and wet. "The warmth is from the bacteria," says Mr. Singh. "If we had started the pile much larger, it would be hotter because it would be less open to the cold air," he says.

Taking Care of Compost

We add more layers of leaves and kitchen scraps. We don't add water because it rained two days ago. "Should we turn the compost today?" I ask.

HOW MUCH CARBON, HOW MUCH NITROGEN?

For composting to work, it needs the right amount of carbon and nitrogen sources. This means you need to add plenty of dead leaves to your green plant parts or kitchen scraps.

Gardeners check their compost piles to make sure they are working properly.

"I don't think so," replies Mr. Singh. "The bacteria aren't quite finished inside the pile. We'll let them finish. We'll know they are done when the pile cools. Then we'll turn it to give them the material on the edges of the pile." ★

Mr. Singh and I are visiting his friend Sam, who lives in an apartment. Sam says he composts to make rich soil for his potted plants. He also says he wants to send less garbage to the landfill. Sam makes special compost in a small covered box in the apartment.

Worms at Work

The compost is made by bacteria and small red worms. Sam is changing his compost today. We watch him push the old compost and worms to one side, add a bedding of

HEALTHY WORMS

Earthworms are necessary to keep soil healthy. Earthworms tunnel through the dirt, making it easier for plants' roots to spread. Worm bodies break down food in the dirt. Not all worms work well in a compost pile. Most worms cannot live if the compost gets too warm. Worms sold for indoor compost are typically small red worms that would not survive well outside in the garden.

Worms can make their own body weight in compost every day.

shredded paper, and then mix in kitchen scraps. Sam says the worms will move from the old compost into the new bedding to break it down. Then, Sam will be able to take the compost out of the composter and use it for his plants. In an indoor composter, worms can produce their weight in compost every day. ★

My compost pile has been going for one month now. Mr. Singh and I are adding another layer of kitchen scraps and grass clippings for nitrogen. We also add another layer of dried leaves for carbon. Before we add the new layers, we look into the pile. A lot of the things we put into it have disappeared. Things have become black, crumbly, and hard to recognize. We find earthworms, beetles, and insects. Mr. Singh says these all come to the compost to eat, and they break down plant material from large pieces to smaller ones. ★

ANIMALS THAT COMPOST

Humans are not the only composters. The Australian brush turkey builds a large pile of decomposing brush and leaves. The compost keeps the brush turkey's eggs warm. The turkey changes the size of its compost heap to create the right temperature for its eggs. Likewise, the American alligator builds a nest of soil and water plants. Decomposing plants warm the alligator's eggs.

Gardeners stir up their compost so everything breaks down evenly.

I am reporting from the city landfill just outside of town. The manager of the City Compost Facility, Mr. Alfred Gonzalez, is giving me a tour. This is composting on a huge scale. The large yard is filled with long rows of compost 6 feet (1.8 m) high and 200 feet (61 m) long. Mr. Gonzalez calls these compost piles windrows.

To begin my interview, I ask, "Where does all of this stuff come from?"

Many cities and counties have compost programs.

"When people at home put out their yard clippings each week, the trucks bring them here. We also collect all of the waste that city workers make when they cut down trees or landscape a park. We grind everything and then make these windrows. We also mix in sludge from the city's sewage treatment plant," says Mr. Gonzalez.

"You put sewage in the compost?" I ask.

"Yes, but our composting method is very hot. This makes sure that any diseases from the sewage are killed," says Mr. Gonzalez. "The heat also kills weed seeds, so they don't grow when you put the compost on a garden.

"The hot composting method also makes our composting process very fast. It takes about one month

COMPOSTING BY CITIES

The U.S. government estimates that 24 percent of city garbage could be composted. Most of that currently goes into landfills. Many cities do compost, but much more could be done. In 2007, in the state of Ohio, residents recycled or composted 62 percent of yard trimmings and plant materials. However, Ohio residents composted less than 3 percent of their food waste. Individuals can help by composting at home.

Large machines move compost in city compost facilities.

to make compost from start to finish," Mr. Gonzalez
explains over the loud noise of a machine.

"What is that machine?" I ask.

Mr. Gonzalez points to the machine driving along the
windrow with wheels on either side. He says, "That machine
drives along the windrow every three days. It turns over

the compost to mix the materials and mix in air that the bacteria need."

"And where does your compost go?" I ask.

"Some of it is used by the city in our parks. The rest we put into bags that you can buy at your garden store."

"You make money with garbage?" I ask.

Looking happily at the steaming windrows, Mr. Gonzalez answers, "We make money, and we save even more money. Some people actually think this is garbage!" ★

COLD AND HOT BACTERIA

Different groups of bacteria and fungi work in different temperatures of compost. When a compost pile starts, the cold compost is home to cold-loving bacteria that live best at temperatures up to 70°F (21°C). These bacteria cause slow rotting. When the compost pile begins to warm, the cold-loving bacteria die and warm-loving bacteria take over. The warm-loving bacteria like temperatures from 70°F to 90°F (21°C to 32°C). When a compost pile becomes very hot, the heat-loving bacteria take over. Heat-loving bacteria can survive in temperatures up to 160°F (71°C).

MISSION ACCOMPLISHED!

Congratulations! You have uncovered the secrets of compost. Composting is a natural way to get rid of food and yard waste. Composting uses organisms called decomposers, including bacteria and fungi, to break down kitchen and garden wastes into smaller parts. The result of composting is rich humus with nutrients and minerals for plants. A compost pile needs carbon and nitrogen to feed bacteria and fungi. Hot composting works quickly and kills diseases and weed seeds. Cold composting makes compost just as well as hot composting. Composting keeps garbage out of landfills, making them last longer. Composting can be done by an entire city, in the backyard of a home, on a balcony, or inside an apartment. Compost provides nutrients for gardens or potted plants.

CONSIDER THIS

Consider the benefits of starting your own compost pile. By asking yourself more questions about compost, you might just start a mission of your own!

What do you throw away that could be composted?

★ How is composting similar to recycling?

★ How can composting preserve land that could be used for other purposes?

★ In what other ways might composting benefit people, plants, and animals?

★ What do you throw away that you could compost?

bacteria (bak-TIHR-ee-uh) tiny living things that can be seen only with a microscope

carbon (KAR-bohn) a chemical element; for composting, carbon comes from tough plant materials

cellulose (SEL-yuh-lohss) a fiberlike chemical found in plants

decompose (dee-kuhm-POZE) to break down into smaller pieces

fungi (FUHN-jye) a plantlike thing with no roots or leaves; molds and mushrooms are fungi

landfill (LAND-fil) an area of low-lying land filled with layers of trash and dirt

molecule (MOL-uh-kyool) the smallest part of a substance; almost everything is made of molecules

nitrogen (NYE-truh-juhn) a chemical element; for composting, nitrogen comes from food scraps, manure, or green plant cuttings

nutrient (NOO-tree-uhnt) a mineral or a chemical needed by a living thing to stay healthy

organism (OR-guh-niz-uhm) a living thing

protein (PROH-teen) a chemical in living things that contains nitrogen

LEARN MORE

BOOKS

Chappell, Rachel. *What's Going on in the Compost Pile?: A Book About Systems (Big Ideas for Young Scientists)*. Vero Beach, FL: Rourke Publishing, 2008.

Cox, Martyn. *Wildlife Gardening*. New York, NY: DK Publishing, 2009.

Silverman, Buffy. *Composting: Decomposition (Do It Yourself)*. Portsmouth, NH: Heinemann Educational Books, 2008.

WEB SITES

Composting for Kids.

http://aggie-horticulture.tamu.edu/sustainable/slidesets/kidscompost/cover.html

See a slide show about composting.

Kids Recycle! Composting.

http://www.kidsrecycle.org/composting.php

Get more information about compost.

FURTHER MISSIONS

GET COMPOSTING!

Now you know enough about composting to start your own compost pile. Ask your parents for a good place to put the compost pile. Be sure that you have some of the materials you need before you begin, such as leaves, garden clippings, and kitchen scraps.

If you live in an apartment or have a small yard, it might be easier to start a worm compost bin at home. You could also ask your teacher to help you start a worm compost bin as a class project.

VISIT YOUR LOCAL SEWAGE TREATMENT PLANT OR COMPOSTING FACILITY

Composting happens all around us. Sewage treatment plants use bacteria to treat the wastewater we produce, much like a compost pile decomposes other forms of garbage. Visit your nearest sewage treatment plant to discover how we use bacteria to break down wastes and keep our waterways clean and disease-free. Many city sewage treatment plants have organized tours for the public or for schools. They are more interesting than you might think!

INDEX

ABOUT THE AUTHOR

David Barker obtained his doctorate in zoology at the University of Texas at Austin. Since then, Dr. Barker has taught and worked as an editor and writer of educational products in print and on the Internet. He lives in Texas and in his spare time makes photographs using historical methods.

ABOUT THE CONSULTANTS

Karen O'Connor is a gardening and local food advocate from Minnesota. She is co-owner of Mother Earth Gardens in Minneapolis, an independent garden center focusing on organic and sustainable gardening. She lives with her husband, two sons, and several small pets.

Gail Saunders-Smith is a former classroom teacher and Reading Recovery teacher leader. Currently she teaches literacy courses at Youngstown State University in Ohio. Gail is the author of many books for children and three professional books for teachers.